Under the Weight of Heaven

Under the Weight of Heaven

Writing from
the Abbey of Gethsemani

Trappist, Kentucky

Edited by John B. Lee

Black Moss Press

2008

Library and Archives Canada Cataloguing in Publication

Under the weight of Heaven : writing from the Abbey of
Gethsemani / edited by John B. Lee.

Poems.
ISBN 978-0-88753-453-9

1. Monastic and religious life--Poetry. 2. Abbey of Our Lady
of Gethsemani (Trappist, Ky.)--Poetry. 3. Christian poetry,
Canadian (English). 4. Canadian poetry (English)--21st
century. I. Lee, John B., 1951-

PS8287.R4U53 2008   C811'.60803823   C2008-903085-0

Cover Design: Caitlin Shaw

Published by Black Moss Press, 2450 Byng Road, Windsor,
Ontario N8W 3E8. Black Moss Press books are distributed by
LitDistco, and all orders should be directed there.

Black Moss acknowledges the generous support for its
publishing program from The Canada Council for the Arts and
The Ontario Arts Council.

The Canada Council | Le Conseil des Arts
for the Arts | du Canada

ONTARIO ARTS COUNCIL
CONSEIL DES ARTS DE L'ONTARIO

Table of Contents

Acknowledgements

"But Where Were the Horses of Evening" first appeared in the book of the same title *(Serengeti Press, 2007)* and reappears here with permission of Serengeti

"Attentive Waiting" first appeared in the book **Left Hand Horses: meditations on influence and the imagination** *(Black Moss Press, 2007) and reappears here with permission of Black Moss*

an excerpt from **Last Labour of the Heart** *appeared in the novel of the same title (Black Moss Press, 2006) and reappears here with permission of the author and Black Moss*

Foreword

"There must be a middle place between abstraction and childishness where one can talk seriously about serious things."
"Treatise on Theology" Czeslaw Milos

Perhaps there are sacred places where the spirit briefly feels at home, as it is, when in solitude and silence, we catch a momentary glimpse of grace while we vanish into the ever-present presence of absence.

Where is this holy ground? What is this blessed state? The seeker seems bereft, surrenders as he fails, then stumbles into beauty like a careless child into an unmarked well. It happens when he pays attention to the whereabouts of loss. It occurs when the heart becalms, the mind believes, the body beholds, and the soul becomes in the spirit fold of fully imagined and thereby reified truth that achieves the connection between the inner-life and outer-world of the otherwise disconnected "I". Thus we know the covenant. Thus the alienated predicament of the individual human self might reconnect with the eternal and the universal holiness of being alive.

*

There is a photograph of fellow traveler, poet Roger Bell, and me, leaning on a garden wall situated outside of the Abbey of Gethsemani. The words *God Alone* are engraved in the stone edifice by the gate. We have the nonchalance of those unaware of the camera's presence. We are indeed the best of friends, this atheist and I. The walkway leading to the chapel divides the silent sanctuary of the cloister walk from the graveyard and beyond the graves the road. It was exactly there that we encountered Trappist monk Brother Paul Quenon for the first time. Brother Paul greeted us

9

with a warm embrace saying, "Welcome! You're so lucky to be here now. Brother Aelred just died and you'll be able to witness a genuine Trappist funeral.

His salutation was engaging and full of joy. We found it strange, but then perhaps, we thought, there is something to be said for welcoming death with such enthusiasm. After all, who else, if not a monk, might have faith that in death, the afterlife welcomes the dying man into paradise.

Brother Aelred's story involved spending the last several years in self-imposed isolation sitting alone in a chair at his bedside in a monastic room. He died seated, his knees bent, his posture frozen in that state. And so, there he was now, lying flat on his back under his winding sheet at the front of the chapel his knees permanently cocked like a dog asleep, his face a rugged stone-cut profile otherwise hidden by the odd body-follow of his shroud, as one monk among sequence of monks sat nearby for the necessary three day and three night vigil.

"Isn't it wonderful," Brother Paul said.

And then, three days later, in the excruciating torpor of a 104 degree Kentucky summer day, we witnessed our first, last, and only Trappist funeral. Wrapped in his winding sheet, Brother Aelred was lowered onto the floor of his pine-bough-lined grave. Up from the hole by way of a ladder came the monk in charge of retrieving the sling ropes. Following the seemingly endless ceremony the priests filed back into the chapel. They were the most rubicund-visaged holy men I have ever seen. Red from the heat of the sun and the unforgiving swelter of their sweat-heavy robes, their hands dripping from the sleeves of their cassocks like fire-softened wax, they suffered their duty and went in.

I have now had the privilege of returning to Gethsemani on five separate occasions. Brother Paul Quenon and I have become friends. In 2001 we collaborated as co-editors on an anthology called, Smaller Than God: words of spiritual longing, wherein we brought together works of poetry and prose in an effort to provide a communion between spiritual atheists and true believers.

During my sojourns at Gethsemani I have stayed in residence at a place I call *the monk motel* because it is comprised of a strip of rooms looking very much like those found at a roadside inn. I have stayed in a building called 'the studio', and I have stayed in the main monastery. It was while staying at the monk motel that I witnessed Roger Bell and Brother Paul Quenon playing garbage lid Frisbee. It was while staying at the studio that Roger Bell and I were visited by a bluebird. Roger and I had been commiserating. He was lamenting the fact that he had not seen a bluebird since his Port Elgin childhood. I was saying that I had never seen a bluebird. And then, at that exact moment a bluebird landed at the edge of the bean field right in front of us as if conjured by our conversation. It was also here that I saw horses the following morning. And while staying in the monastery proper, I was visited one night in a dream by demons and another night by angels.

When I went to bed, I felt very ill at ease. I did not feel that I belonged inside the walls in this hot cloister room. I felt unworthy of the honour of being in the sleeping company of devout monks. To make matters worse, the electric fan on the chair in my room did not work. I fell asleep in the humid and stuffy room and woke suddenly with a start feeling myself enmeshed in a drifting-down veil of dark demons amorphous as smoke smoldering up from my body. More real than any nightmare, I knew if I failed to wake I was doomed. As I emerged from the fog of sleep, I shook away the blur as one might kick a fever-heated blanket to the floor.

The following night I woke at 23 minutes past the hour every hour from 11:23 till morning. I glanced at the face beside the bed and saw the blazing red brand of the travel clock burning those numbers on my sleepy retina.

When I told Brother Paul of my strange experience he confirmed that it was entirely possible that I had been visited by evil spirits and on the second night by angels.

"Why angels?" I asked.

"Because angels love symmetry," he replied.

A year later, after thinking about his statement concerning angels, I asked, "Brother Paul, how do you know angels love symmetry?"

"I don't," he said. "I just made it up." At which he smiled mischievously.

And so Gethsemani has been for me one of those sacred places, place of demons and angels, a place for serious contemplation and for light-hearted confabulation.

The last time there, I was with my wife, Cathy, on a short stop over on our way south. Meeting Cathy for the first time, Brother Paul said to her, "You are so natural. It is wonderful that John has someone down to earth like you to keep him grounded."

Just before he said that, we had been talking about getting older and how perhaps most of us age without becoming wise. Some of us are fortunate to be blessed by improvements in our virtues, but at the same time we are cursed by the deepening of our flaws. Or so suggested Brother Paul.

We departed musing on such thoughts when we suddenly found ourselves lost in the quickly falling dark on a back road only a mile from the monastery. We pulled into the driveway at a house in the fork in the road to ask directions. A young man had just gotten home and was only nicely out of his truck. "Ask that man for directions," my wife said.

I opened the door and stepped out of the vehicle saying, "Excuse me, sir …"

The young man flew into a rage and started screaming,

"Fuck off! Get the fuck off my land!" He turned on his heel and ran into the house slamming the door. He quickly came back brandishing something I didn't quite see which may or may not have been a gun.

Needless to say, we fled the scene brutalized and in shock. We sped along the road not looking back wondering how this sort of behaviour could occur in such close proximity to such a sacred place. This young man almost completely destroyed the good mood and here only a short distance from sacred ground stood this dark place.

*

"We live here under the weight of heaven too often with heavy hearts striking in our breasts like angry stones," I thought.

And yet, I believe in the transformative power of poetry and prayer. May these poems and stories reclaim some of the good even from the darker angels of our worsened Nature.

John B. Lee

Awakening

Brother Paul Quenon

Muffled lowing of a cow
sends mother-comfort to
the hermit asleep
under a full moon.

Strangeness! Strangeness!
The owl cries
to the frosted world.

"That's a dog howling."
The monk awakened says.
Strangeness! Strangeness!
He goes back to sleep.

*

Nighttime troubadours
circle through woods and fields
—hounds singing hound love.

*

A mule cried at night:
"I, I am the only mule!"
Then from a distance
another mule cried:
"I am the only mule—I!"
Then the night went mute.

*

Webs of clouds weave dreams
across the face of the moon
—sleeping, half smiling.

Send my stuff

Roger Bell

When I left the north
it was cool but dry
the corn was tall
the children contented

I intended to return

but
down here things are different
genteelly overgrown, dripping
lush and slow as the green rivers

there is no simple explanation
trying would be futile
you will be wounded
and cry, no matter how
much I want you not to
so

send my stuff
send it south
excise all of me
from your lives
I don't exist
and never did.

First Gethsemani Morning

Hugh MacDonald

As I tiptoe out past the others
that first morning at the Abbey
the dense fog of early morning
is a delicate tatting of liquid lace
on the face of a dawning landscape
close and suffocating, and I tumble
from the air-conditioned studio
into this startling greenhouse heat
a reversal for this northern boy
in to out, where the trees that ring
the small pond are lichen hung
and moist bean fields stretch outward
fade into creamy cloud in the distance
and I am on an early morning island
green like my own, but a foreign land.
And here in this Trappist's paradise
I open myself to hot succulent air
feel vestiges of long-severed roots
seek out the broken pots of memory.
At Compline, seductive chants and psalms
and I remember youthful blindness
and a certain faith they warned me
I might someday lose forever
those dark-robed Redemptorists
whose pale, thin hands I washed
and whose sweet communion wine
I helped to thin with grudging water
but still, here in this verdant garden
there is something hard to leave
the happiness that defined my youth
hand in hand with overwhelming fear

that never made sense by light of day
but still arises like mists to haunt by night.

hawk

mary ann mulhern

in the mist of morning
when monks answer bells
a hawk circles
above monastary trees
wings spread in glory
talons bared
to grasp a newborn rabbit
tear a heart from life
even here
in the silence of centuries
blood spills
over stones of peace

Mountain Climbing

Brother Paul Quenon

I set out alone towards the east,
walking in a summer afternoon
on a secret trail through
a grassy forgotten valley
and find my way to a mountain
that no one knows about.
I have been here before,
explored alone the route
that only I know. It is very familiar
though changed—

always familiar, though
never twice the same.
I have the energy
to take the long irregular climb.

I arrive at the summit
totally alone. Something absolute
grips my senses. I all but breathe it in.
I have been here, I know
I have been here before.

The descent glides past
a wooded meadow
to the monastery, where
I will be happy to show
it to others.

I awake.
It is dark.
My sense of the summit
begins to fade, as always.
But this time I will
help it stay.

I walk it in the dark.
Alone, after Laud,
towards wintry hills,
distant silhouettes,
confident on the pale road
in the memory,
—summit beyond no more
than shadow and sky.

It is enough.

Cape Sable

Robert Hill

A monk might find comfort here.
  The light is all the same
    Sea, Sky
  endless miles of sand—
  A monotony of light.
Yes, this might please a monk who,
  praying for mindless life,
  would find fulfillment in
  a landscape stretching forever.
    Except
  it is deception.
In losing mind, we lose connection.
In lost connection, we close the door to peace.
  Those monks—deserters from the world.
    Mea Culpa!
Best to say it loudly and have good reason for it
  This sitting on a cloister fence
  not here—not there
  neither in this world or the world to come.
  Commit yourself and be honest.
  No senseless fabrication
    No.
  We lose the mind
  and then the light
  and then the heart.
An annulled marriage to the world
  saying offices
with the sad patterns of a deserted soul.
  Life is lived by living
  without which we cannot die.

Lilacs of Kentucky

Marilyn Gear Pilling

You climb the split rail fence, balance on top, tip
        your head back, reach towards heaven, wobble
                in a swim of scent that nearly drowns you,
                    breathe in.

The cascade of memory catches in your hair; instantly
        you see your mother and her sisters, the three of them
        looking a little old-fashioned now, their house-dresses
                of tiny, flowered print, their home-done perms.

You yearn to gather them, the purple panicles, the fresh
        green hearts,
                the little twigs, your mother and your aunts,
                        take them as you would gather harvest grasses,
                            armfuls and armfuls.

You want to bring them in, whelm of their scent against
        your face
                settle them in a blue delft pitcher, let them
                saturate the air
                        you breathe, knowing where they will take you,
                                knowing what you risk.

Storm over Kentucky

Roger Bell

Around eleven it moved in
a muscled push
cool wind
over the plush western hills
then on its heels
a throat-clearing pronouncement
a brilliant ion-charged flare.

As I bid you goodnight
and stepped sleepily barefoot
to turn out the lights, I trod
on a nasty bit of glass.
My blood welled black but
I staunched it
with pressure and pent-up breath
though the storm would not be so easily quelled
the rain burst
as even the stars were drowned
and the katydid choir
washed to silence.

Over this Gethsemani, this God's garden
it was a relentless night
through drawn blinds, fragments
of white light invaded, and I dreamed
of you as faceless
your voice the unremitting wind.
The air conditioner howled
and pumped sweat so
twist-soaked sheets twined
like serpents about my legs.

With dawn's hesitation I staggered awake
where the last shreds of cloud
draped immodestly over
the indecent early day
and mist obscured the bells of the monastery.

You told me that
I'd been speaking in tongues
that you had grown afraid.
When I showed you my foot
again, gushing
and the other, and my palms
all wounded now
you withdrew, knelt, crossed yourself
began to pray, vigorously.

I don't know, here and now
who I am
but I am far from home
there is no solace
in the cruciform on the hill
or in the morning stir
of breakfast table voice
I am forsaken

and I bleed
oh, God
how I bleed.

Basil's Lake

Roger Bell

The red-tailed hawk, gyring
thinks we're fools
he has more important things than
three grey-bearded boys
paddling naked in Basil's Lake
with swallowtails and damsel flies
dappling the day.

He has more pressing business
ignores
the white moons we display
at the sky
as we dive
down
where the spring feeds
cool below the sun-warmed surface
down through the years
then languidly drift back
to the unpressing present.
He hasn't taken our vow of lassitude
this hawk, nonetheless
descends to investigate
the laughter like silver fish
rippling his lake
circles, looks
then knowing he was right
dismisses
pumps
and kicks up again
into the steaming air
rides the updraft
of his industry.

He sleeps outdoors year-round

Roger Bell

There are no ceilings between Paul and God
as he reclines in the cicada-laden night
where he sees amazed the firmament wheel
where he keeps track of the Lord's wristwatch
wound every day on the stem of what's real.

But Where Were the Horses of Evening

John B. Lee

The horses are eating the fogs of the dawn
it has whitened their bones
like birches, their hearts become
stone under foam
they drum to the withers
in rivers of burning
they come to the fences
a-smoulder and vanish
like blown-away breath
in the vapour of naming
their manes
like what clings
to the sashes worn ragged
at the fringes of windows
of houses
they stand
in wet grasses
brown-girthed to grey vapour
as if they were floating

great boats of bent ribs
arriving or leaving
adrift on far meadows
grown calm after heaving
and slowing their breathing ...

last night
was loneliness lovely outside
by the bean field
the fireflies flickered
like stars we were dreaming
friend Roger in doorlight
while old heaven showed
in the wet of the pond
how it was
aging with faith in the failures
of moonlight forgetful
in cloud-cross like losses
from memory sleeping

but where were the horses
of morning—I wonder
where were they waiting
what elsewhere was in them
what linger of distant green hunger
the grasses were building
from darkness
to bless us in daylight
to fill our sad bodies
like vases of silence
with silence

Under the Weight of Heaven

for Paul Quenon
Marty Gervais

You sleep in the tool shed
by the road under the stars
at the back of the monastery
and tell me about the lovers
—the farm boys
with their sweethearts
who steal into the night
when all is asleep here
and park their cars
in the holy stillness
and after a while
quietly drive back out
to the highway.
You hear their cars
mounting the hill beyond
and hear them disappear into
the splendid darkness
You sleep in the tool shed
by the road under the stars
and awake suddenly to
an unfamiliar sound
on the road
and look up and see
the enormous shape
of a horse like a mountain
emerging from the mist
in the early morning

but only a horse
a mare that has strayed from

a nearby farm
It lolls about
under the swaying weight
of the heavens
You sleep in the tool shed
by the road
under the stars
and wake to the morning
with the bells beckoning you
to vigils—then you see
this work horse lying
in the dark meadow
and nod to her as you would
a friend, and say good morning
You sleep in the tool shed
under the stars
where the world
comes to you
—silent guests who steal away
your sleep, who leave you
wondering, who leave you
undisturbed, alone
You sleep in the tool shed
under the weight of Heaven ...

At Merton's Hermitage

Hugh MacDonald

Five poets sit
in a sort of symmetry
our awkward placement of hands
reading like young actors
unused to the stage
suspended somewhere between
giddiness and serenity.
How like boys we are
our casual shoes
our worn blue jeans
John B. somewhat
Out-of-sync in green
our dew stained cuffs
soaked while sponging
through full blown
wild Kentucky grass
after Gethsemane's
massive breakfast of porridge
and eggs, jams and jellies
clumps of peanut butter
racks of perfect toast
steaming cups of tea
then, the air alive
with butterflies and gnats
Brother Paul
and Marty in the lead
John inquiring after
leaf and blade of grass
we stroll a swath
like Merton cut
through domesticated wild places
from the working monastery

to his Hermitage on the hill.
We look about inside
meditate on this concrete cell
that briefly housed
the soul that was his life
our gift the sharing
of his human frailties
his familiar temptations
his hypnotic soaring range of words
We humbly sit at this shrine
while below us the long view
spans acres of wood and grass
the downward sloping field before
bends toward the world's gate
our thoughts for the moment
temperate and peaceful
reflect the shimmer of summer
the shade tree beyond the porch
while behind us the empty bed
where Merton slept and didn't
where within him wrestled
the love of internal peace
the turmoil of animal joy
the mad man-parts
that we all share
the saints we sometimes are
the beasts we can become
the blackened hearth
that conjures fiery pits
and writhing monsters
that we still smell today
separated by time and space
thankful for each garnered day
for light upon awakening
in dread of one last morning
that ends abruptly in darkness.

Pilgrimage to Prades, France

Marilyn Gear Pilling

On the last day of January 1915,
under the sign of the Water Bearer,
in a year of a great war,
and down in the shadow of some French
mountains on the borders of Spain,
I came into the world.

Thomas Merton, Seven Storey Mountain

Whether the sun is in the dazzle sky of showoff blue
or the moon is in the boudoir sky of throbbing black

whether crazy sidewalks hopscotch to the end of town
or tilt towards the green valley

whether poppies shout from the orange ditches
or Spain thrums behind the lavender mountains

whether Christ bleeds marble from His forehead
or sidewalks flaunt their coprophiliac delight

whether breadsticks poke insouciant from baskets
or tatterdemalions flap at birds in orchards

whether blue coos of mourning doves
taupe dog waggle
purple tantrums of church bells
wanton carmine tablecloths
hullaballooning on clotheslines
orange cats curled among loaves in sunshine

no matter the revelation
          I behold the seeds
                 of yourcontemplation.

Walking in Thomas Merton's Boots

for Brother Anthony
Marty Gervais

The field outside is soggy with January rain rendering my
street shoes useless and so I reach for a pair of rubber
boots by the door only to find three left-fitting galoshes,
one right. Someone's walked off with two rights or so
it would appear. What's with this place? Everything
is labeled *Merton's Water, Merton's Gloves, Merton's Ax.*
Everything else must be mine. Who is this Merton? A
question he probably needed to answer himself ... It
occurs to me as I push my feet into the rubber boots and
step out into the dampness leaving behind two lefts that
Merton's out there somewhere—walking
around with two right-fitting boots marked legibly *Merton's
Boots.*

The photographer and the Virgin

for all mothers and sons
Roger Bell

Sorry, Mary
he whispers
steps
up onto her pedestal
to shoot red morning
birthing itself in the mist
above the still sleeping abbey

he embraces her
and she him
her weathered arms
so long without love

every bit the wanderer
weary from the road
he lays his chin
upon her shoulder
and there rests long moments, focusing
her lips so very near his ear
her breathing barely dew

the way he holds the moment
the way she holds her boy
allows the shutter to relax
so the picture then completes itself

the past winging like night into the west
forgiven
mother and son
then and now
as one

Playing garbage can lid frisbee with a monk in 100 degree sunshine

Roger Bell

you'll probably get cholera
but once you push past
the stench of the green flying saucer
learn to absorb the weight
ignore the scratch of sweat at your eyes and
the underwear riding the crack of your ass

you realize
maybe you still can learn
when you throw caution
unwieldy and strange
wobbling
into the eager wind

Stuffed Dog

for Paul Quenon
Roger Bell

I will steal that stuffed dog
from the lawn where he has long languished
from his locked gaze on the carpassing days and

I don't care whose shotgun blast tells me I can't
I will

and I will take him from this oppressive heat
this steamy relentless eye of sun

flee Kentucky and Ohio
cross the border at Detroit smuggler brave
Don't touch him, officer, he's rigid with fear
and though he's not a biter, well...

into the release of Canada, where the air dances lighter
than a grey squirrel through oak leaves
and I'll roll down the window and stick his head out
and step on the gas so his ears blow back
and the wind sings a familiar dog song
and his plugged nostrils open
as his neck unlocks and he turns to me
and we both, giddy, on the unleashed highway
tilt back our heads and howl

On the Outskirts of Gethsemani

Hugh MacDonald

On several occasions as we drive
between Bardstown and the Monastery
we glide past the Bluegrass Tavern
and more than once Marty says:
I've always wanted to go in there.
And this time I ask why don't we
and Roger says because he's only wearing
sandals and they're useless in a brawl
he left his Doc Martens at home
and we laugh, four poets in black T's
brazen Canada flags across our smug
chests, red as bleeding hearts, mouth
raspberries at the unschooled red-necked
patrons we imagine inside. But John B

stops and parks and we creep inside this
foreign murk, superior northern lungs
braving the choke of cigarette and cigar.
Small hairs dance across napes of our
holier-than-thou necks as curious faces
take their cues, lift from battles of the balls
before them on fields of miniature bluegrass
or turn away from the polished altar
of the bar to watch our alien foursome
slide on past. We find four stools and order
frosted mugs of draft from the warm-voiced
woman behind the bar and John B picks up
a folded section of a local paper that sits
on the bar top before him as if someone knew
what we were thinking. John finds a Latin quote
penned across the upper margin of the page
in an ornate hand and below it the translation
as if the writer knew we'd be impressed by dead tongues
and too long out of school. He shows it to me
and then on another page the word: Metaphysics
followed by an accurate definition. Something
changes in the lighting in the room. We have
a lot to learn I say and turn to my beer. That's
when John B. spotted the starry homage
to Van Gogh at the far end of the tavern,
stretching wall to wall, ceiling to floor.
He nudged me and pointed, his mouth hanging
open as a human giant with exophthalmic eyes
rose up, huge feet scraping slow as twin bulldozers
toward us. Inches from John, he stops and stares
past us as though we are fog and we wonder
what comes next, was Roger right after all?
Has he taken exception to our shirts, our mean
Joe Weider disdain for Charles Atlas to the south.
The hulk stands silent several nervous seconds

and then begins a slow Kentucky drawl
tells how he retired and bought this place
remembered certain paintings by Van Gogh
from a book and fell in love and how he thought
they would look real good on a wall lit up
in black light. And how just at the right moment
a guy who had done all kinds of art work
for Disney moved up to Kentucky and didn't
have time to paint a wall but his son might
and did. The way the kid mixed the paint under black
light and made it look layered, the way Van Gogh
made it thick by laying on coat after coat of paint.
He sways ploddingly down with us to view his
Starry Night and The Potato Eaters on one side wall
and other velvety Van Gogh's across the way. We return
to our seats and our big friend joins us and we
talk like older men who've been friends forever
compare medications and even show scars, drink
cold Kentucky beers and feel like we're close to home.

Sts. Gervaise and Protais

for Marty Gervais
Brother Paul Quenon

St. Gervaise, your martyred patron, was, according to
the New Catholic Encyclopaedia, a big unidentified
corpse buried next to another oversized corpse, whose
lives according to sound historical criticism are forever
unknown, and whose deaths are no longer certain to be
by martyrdom.

So you Marty, an expert on 'the science of nothing', do

well to be guarded by a saint whose very reputation is nullified.

Every time you lapse into self doubt, you could be sinking into the arms of a patron non-saint who may not even have arms.

History does know an ampulla was certainly buried with them, which seems perfect, since you don't likely know what an ampulla is any more than I did. But don't look up the word, it has four definitions and you might be thinking—like it was a vessel for Eucharistic wine. But they just might have been drinking buddies and big bruisers fell down dead drunk and got buried that way— happily enough, let's say.

In a Garden of Lies

for Marty Gervais
Brother Paul Quenon

Plato, as you know
wanted to kick the poets out of town
for being such liars!

Monks flee the cities
to get away from lies.
So why does a poet like you
leave town and come to the monastery?
It makes me wonder.

I, myself, instinctively mistrust
whoever swears up and down

they are telling the solemn truth.
You swear up and down
you are telling professional lies.
So maybe I half-way trust you.
At least you keep truth on a human scale.

God alone
in our oblique theology
tells lies on a grand scale.
Every word and event a
disguise of the Unpronounceable.

I turn the leaves of
your latest volume rich with
act-dumb complacency
over what, ultimately,
neither one of us
has yet to see.

Better to keep it that way, Marty.
Better to keep it that way.

The Boy with the Book on His Head

John B. Lee

my mother was teaching her daughter
the elegant posture of girls
though my sister walked
with a sway in her spine
mother said—straighten your back
to the door
and I'll measure your worth
with a mark
for your height and your growth in the day

and she placed on the round
of her hair
a copy of thought
and said, walk without spilling the words
as if she were
come from a well
with a jug of old sky
to sweeten the thirst of her home
with a portable potable blue
and it spilled
like the flight of a bird
its fluttering pages
like wings
as it breathed to the floor
with a thump
and a clop that went red
for its covers were red
an unreadable red
like the unwanted blushing of love
or the blood of our Lord
in the wine

and so I said
mother, miter me with
that sensible hat

and she set me the task
and I strode
and was straight in my care
like those who suffer from aches in their bones
or those who
are old on the ice

and I felt myself
crowned by a book
and I danced on the floor
like the dream of a dog
and I flickered like feathers in flame

but what of my sister
poor girl
she caught my cool shadow
in play
like the darkness of shadow in shade

and what might I say
that I'm sorry
for being
the boy with the book on his head

I'll just
sit in the corner and *be*

Guardian Angel

Marty Gervais

He's lazy and never around
when I need him
I drive down
to the coffee shop
in the early morning
and find him reading the paper
or talking to the locals
I want to tell him
he's not taking this seriously
—he's supposed to watch over me
He shrugs and says the rules
have changed
I can reach him on *Facebook*
Besides he carries a cell phone
I want to ask how he got this job
Why me? Why him?
Luck of the draw, he shrugs
our birthdays the same
we both have bad eyes
a hearing problem
and can't eat spicy foods
But where was he in October 1950
the afternoon on Wyandotte
when I was four
and I ran between
two parked cars?
He was there, he says
coming out of the pool hall
to save me
to cup my bleeding head
on the warm pavement

to glare at the driver
who stood in the open door
of his Ford worried sick
that I might die
I was there, he said,
otherwise we might not
be having this conversation
and he was there again
when I lay curled up
and unconscious
in the hospital room one winter
swearing at the hospital staff
after bowel surgery
and he touched my lips
with his index and middle fingers
and quieted me
Besides, he's always there
and there's no point
having this conversation
—he's so far ahead
and knows so much more:
a hundred different languages
names of every star
in the universe, the physics
of flying, and the winner
of the Stanley Cup
every year till the
end of time

An excerpt from *The Last Labour of the Heart*:

Paul Vasey

Ten minutes later - three minutes past one - Benjamin was parking the rental car by the side of the road which circled Lake Harriet. There are dozens of lakes in Minneapolis - Benjamin thought it one of the loveliest cities he'd seen - and this little lake a couple of miles from Lou's home was one of his favourites. He locked the car and pocketed the keys, crossed the road and sat on a bench, facing the water.

Their bench: his and Lou's.

Every summer, the past twenty summers, he and Lou had driven to the lake; sat and watched the sun play on the water, the clouds drift past in the blue beyond; listened to the children, listened to the birds; listened to their thoughts; listened to each other. Their last visit, this past summer, they'd idled around the lake, just more than a mile; passed the botanical gardens and the concert shell, the ice-cream shop near which the sailboats were moored to their buoys in the bay. Then they'd circled a second time so Lou could see it all from a different perspective, shadows and sunlight, and make up her mind: butterscotch or chocolate mint.

Then they drove around the lake again, parked in their usual spot, crossed the road to their bench beside the walking trail beside the shore - Lou holding onto her cone with one hand and Benjamin's arm with her other; Benjamin holding up his ice-cream cone, traffic-cop style, to stop oncoming cars as he and Lou turtled across the road.

This is perfect, Lou had thought.

And despite the fact Lou's feet didn't quite touch the earth when she had adjusted herself comfortably on the bench - had she shrunk? or had she always been this small?

- it really was a perfect place to spend an hour of a summer afternoon. For quite some time after settling on the bench they didn't talk much: remarking on a sailboat lazing along the far shore, the beauty - or otherwise - of the dogs, which trotted along beside their owners, tongues damply lolling.

It was one of these dogs - a chocolate Lab named Abby - that had got Lou going on the subject of dogs. As soon as the owner unhooked its leash, the Lab bounded over the low retaining wall and made a dash across the beach to the lake, landing with a splash in front of Benjamin and Lou.

Lou loved Labs. She and Robert had one - this was a long time ago, two or three years after they were married. They'd moved from Manhattan to a farmhouse out in Jersey. It seemed like something out of a storybook at first. They'd rented the house and bought Chester. They stayed in the country a little less than a year. Robert loved it at first but had come - especially that first winter - to hate commuting. So they moved back to Manhattan the following summer. It had broken their hearts to have to leave the dog behind, but they had no choice. Chester was a country dog. He was accustomed to the run of the fields around the farmhouse. He would have hated city life, hated life in an apartment. Robert had been right about that. So they left Chester at the neighbouring farm and drove off. They couldn't look back once they'd started to drive away and it took them quite a long while (two more moves, the second bringing them to Minneapolis) before Lou could bring herself to hang the black and white framed photograph of Chester on the kitchen wall (a snapshot now hanging above the bureau in her little apartment in The Home.) Having that dog, Lou thought, was a little like having a baby - almost - Labs being so bright and curious and affectionate. When Robert got up and went from one room to the next, Chester got up and followed. When Lou went out to the yard to do a bit of gardening, Chester flopped on the grass nearby. When Lou and Robert sat on the loveseat in the evening reading their books, listening to their records, Chester positioned himself so that he could touch both of them: chin on Robert's foot, a paw on Lou's. It sounded hopelessly sentimental to say so, Lou said with an embarrassed smile, but that dog - within days of their bringing him home - had become the light of their lives. Robert used to joke that I was getting to love the dog more than I loved him.

Lou wondered whether, when she got to Heaven - assuming she would get to Heaven - Chester would be waiting with all the other to welcome her. She turned to Benjamin: do you think dogs get to go to Heaven?

That hadn't been something Benjamin had spent much time thinking about. Taking another lick of his cone he asked for a moment to consider it. During that moment, Abby The Lab, who had started all this speculation, bounded out of the lake, came dripping across the grass and - standing directly in front of Benjamin and Lou - gave himself a thorough shake, splattering them both, The owner was profusely apologetic but by this time Lou was scratching the offender under the chin, then feeding him the pointy end of her cone, then giving him a pat on his water-beaded head. The owner apologized once again. Lou told him not to concern himself, then told him about Chester, told him how she loved Labs generally and Chester specifically, then she scratched the water-dog again and bid the owner and Abby good afternoon and she and Benjamin watched as they made their way down the path and out of sight around a bend.

Well?

Well what?

The question of dogs and Heaven.

Give me a minute, said Benjamin.

A minute later: If Heaven was merely a more perfect

rendering of life here on Earth then obviously it would have to be equipped with dogs, bars and golf courses. If, however, Heaven was a reward for those faithful servants who had clung doggedly - pardon the pun - to their beliefs and to the straight and narrow path, shunning sin, doing good works, leaving the world a better place than they had found it (or, at the very least, no worse than they had found it) then clearly dogs - incapable of moral manoeuvring - couldn`t make the cut.

Lou leapt to Chester's defence: If Heaven was a reward for those who made it through the strait gate then clearly Chester would be there, wagging his tail, waiting for her. What kind of Heaven - and reward - would it be if the faithful got there and found their most treasured companions- two legs or four - were not there as well? Benjamin conceded the point. There would be dogs in Heaven. No cats, however.

Lou was with him there.

Winded by their adventures in theology, they sat in silence for another ten or fifteen minutes, listening to the birds, listening to the children playing on the beach, watching the boats and the sun glinting on the waves which lapped on the shore near where they sat - prompting him to think of that line in a Bruce Cockburn song:

All the diamonds in this world
That mean anything to me
Are conjured up by wind and sunlight
Sparkling on the sea

Lovely, said Lou.

Yes, said Benjamin.

And they went back to their silences; watching the people and the pets walking and jogging along the path which ran between them and the shore.

Why do you think we live? said Lou.

Hmm?

Why do you think we're given a life to live, here on earth? Benjamin was embarrassed to say he'd never thought about it; had merely taken it for granted.

Lou had him scrambling now, wanted to know if he meant he was just cruising through life, more or less unconsciously.

Well, he wouldn't say that, exactly.

What else was he saying if he was saying he'd never bothered to take a few minutes to figure out why he was wandering around here on earth as a human being, rather than spending his days as a stump, say, or a stone?

Well, he said.

Don't obfuscate, said Lou.

Well, he said. Yes. I guess.

Shame on you, she said, giving him a nudge in the ribs.

Well, Mrs. Professor, why are we here?

Lou was not overly enamoured of the Catholic view of things - a little too much hocus-pocus, Latin and incense for her - but she thought Saint Ignatius put his gnarly finger on it when he said that it was all pretty simple: man was created to praise God and serve Him and, in doing so, to save his own soul. She thought - Catholic or not - that sort of summed things up. Thought the long and the short of it was this: life on earth was a kind of test drive. You were plunked down here in this garden of earthly delights and detours and left to wander down this path or that, dodging the Devil, seeking the light at the end of the tunnel. If you avoided the bright lights of temptation and focused on the bright light of redemption, then you get to go to Heaven.

A little Sunday-schoolish, thought Benjamin, and said so. Lou didn't think Saint Augustine overly Sunday-schoolish. Or any of the other great thinkers - from Kierkegaard to Thomas Merton - who thought themselves down the same path toward more or less the same conclusion. Which you would think - another nudge in the ribs - that a Mister

Bachelor of Philosophy ought to know.

Question, said Benjamin. What are you going to miss most, once you're dead?

Nothing, said Lou.

Nothing?

Not a thing.

In Lou's view, everything was going to be a whole lot better and purer and more beautiful and peaceful in the place she was going - the place she was hoping to go - than it ever could be in the place she was shortly to leave. She would be rejoined with those she loved: Mother and Father, the boys and Robert. And you too, she said, turning to face Benjamin. Though I'm in no hurry to see you up there. You can take your time joining me. Eternity lasts quite some time, I'm told. I won't mind waiting a few more years to see you.

Benjamin thought it was gracious of her to say so.

And was reminded of Rilke:

It's very hard to be dead
    And you try
    To make up for lost time
Till slowly you start
    To get whiffs
    Of eternity

I like that, said Lou, with what could only be described as a little-girl smile. I may have to steal it.

Go right ahead, said Benjamin. I did. And speaking of eternity, he wondered what she was going to do with all that time on her hands.

She would think of something. I expect I'll find sufficient to keep me interested. Life in Heaven has to be at least as interesting as life here on earth. And she wouldn't mind have a little sit-down with The Creator, for whom she had a couple of questions.

Such as?

None of your business.

You really do believe in all that, don't you?

All what?

Heaven and God. Angels and eternity. All of that.

Of course, said Lou. She turned a surprised and concerned look upon him. Don't you?

Benjamin wished. He envied Lou her faith and her hope and her confidence. But where Lou saw light, he saw only shadows; while her heart was full of faith his head was full of doubts and confusion.

No, he said, I can't say I do.

Don't you feel the presence of God all around you?

I can't say I do, Lou.

Oh dear.

Oh dear indeed. Benjamin couldn't have said it better or more succinctly himself. It was a pity. He could sense that, simply by listening to people like Lou talking about their relationship with God. they spoke of God the way they would speak of a kindly uncle or a favourite grandfather; someone they knew to be attentive to them and ever watchful over them. On the one hand, he thought it ridiculous and pathetic that people could whittle God down to size and turn him into some kind of sentimental Buddy. But at the same time, he envied their ability to do so, even if they were deluding themselves; envied the comfort they seemed to derive from it all. But try as he might - and he had tried, Lord knows, had gone to church, said his prayers, sung the hymns - he could never entirely put his heart into Nearer My God To Thee. He was always on the outside when it came to God. He'd read the books: in fact, spent a week one summer in the hills of Kentucky at Gethsemani, the monastery where Thomas Merton had found his way and his peace. Spent the week reading Merton, visited the retreat in the woods where Merton had written, thinking to find in the pages of The Seven Storey Mountain, or within the walls of Merton's cabin, some direction, perhaps, for his own spiritual quest. He found in Merton a reference to the theologian Etienne Gilson and Gilson's wonderful conception of God: He is the pure act of existing. Or, as Merton had added: God is Being Itself. And, back to Gilson: that God is beyond any images of Him that we might conjure up, is in fact beyond conceptualizing, is just out there, as Lou said, all around us. Which is a felt thing.

Benjamin was able to understand what Lou and these others were talking about when they spoke so fervently. But understanding didn't help. What they were talking about was not a matter of the intellect, but a matter of faith. Or belief. Kierkegaard's Great Leap. Which was exactly what Lou and these others had taken: like kids in a park, running down the hill, soaring into flight and landing on the far side of the creek. But Benjamin never took that run. He wandered the creek-bank looking for a bridge. He'd never found the bridge, and never would. There were no bridges. Not across that creek. And he'd been in his forties by the time he figured that out.

Benjamin and Lou sat for a long time that day this past summer, staring into their own distances at their own horizons, not saying a word.

Now, these months later, sitting alone where they had sat together, he wasn't so sure he'd been entirely honest.

He rose and began walking along the path bordering the lake.

There were two paths, actually: one for walkers and joggers, the other for cyclists and roller-skaters. Benjamin kept to the path nearer the lake, the one for walker and joggers.

The first few summers he'd come to Minneapolis, Benjamin had been in the habit of jogging. Early each morning, before Lou and Kathleen and the children had wakened, he drove to the lake and park the car and took a slow run around the shore. Those first dawning hours were a magical time of day. He found himself now and then saying a little prayer of thankfulness for the beauty of the morning and the gift of experiencing it. But though he uttered the words, and meant them, he could not have explained, then or now, to whom he was addressing that little prayer. He had no picture of God - certainly not the flowing beard and flashing eyes of the storybook God - any more than he had a sense of God, except that in some way this was a fearsome more than a loving Being. Certainly not Lou's loving God. Lou's God was a comforting and comfortable presence in her life, a presence she apparently felt about her all the time. Which would be some kind of gift, he thought.

But it was not a gift bestowed upon Benjamin Miles. And he was not sure that what he experienced running around the lake those years ago was really the presence of God at all. Maybe it was just a runner's high.

One thing was certain: the feeling he had while running around the lake, or the feeling he had walking in Ojibway Park back home, was not a feeling he could replicate in a church. Churches, with all their rituals and dogmas, left him feeling claustrophobic. How did anyone think that the God which created Heaven and Earth, which was revealed in the great vaulting heavens over our heads, could be stuffed into an airless little box. Even a box with stained-glass windows. How could anyone be deluded enough to think that God could fit into their boxes, or their ideologies? How could anyone experience God in a place so cut off from God's own world of beauty, in a place so musty and droning, so petty and political, was a mystery to Benjamin. How anyone would want to try to do that was beyond him.

Well, Lou had a more charitable view of churches. Churches, she thought, were a place where the hopeful, the hope-filled, could gather together and publicly express their private faith. Yes, she thought, churches were political - petty and political - and the choirs were filled with people who couldn't sing and the pulpits were full of people who loved the sound of their own voices, and the choirmaster ran off with the choirboy. But despite all that, despite all these painfully and obviously human faults, churches were filled with people who, by and large, were doing their best. They were singing as best they could - in tune or otherwise - the praises of their God.

Yes, said Benjamin. He could see her point. All well and good. But this, he thought as he slowly circled the lake, taking in the sun and the sky and the trees, the water and the unexpected warmth of this October day, this was cathedral enough for him. And the only kind that mattered.

vespers

mary ann mulhern

in the shadowlight of candles
monks chant evening prayers
invoke the black madonna
to protect them
against spirits who appear
from underworlds of sleep
their scent familiar
a perilous presence
only the goddess
can dispel
from cold monastary cells
left unlocked

woman in the temple

mary ann mulhern

monks robed
in baptismal white
chant ancient psalms
Moses, David, and Solomon
songs of Zion
of the Kingdom of Yahweh
voices joined as one
praising one God

and I, a woman,
kneel in the sacrificial silence
of centuries
I become smaller,
a bony rib
covered in naked flesh
taken from Adam
given back
as one
belonging to man

for God, Alone

mary ann mulhern

in a monastary chapel
a white-robed monk reads poetry
Edna St. Vincent Millay,
Browning, Blake,
longings of the heart
beating through centuries
rise and fall of pain
white heat of desire

Brother Mark says
there is no death

only a dark passage
like the channel of birth
opening into life

bells from the tower
sound over a graveyard
white crosses
monks who prayed before dawn
wrapped strong hearts in silence
let them bleed into vows
empty into a passage
they could see
opening.

inside monastery gates

mary ann mulhern

along the walkway
to the abbey
i see gravestones
pitted white, faded marble, bronze,
those who lived in town, on farms,
somewhere in between

in my room
eternal tones of gray
a window over
a monastary graveyard
small white crosses
Michael, Thomas, Charles,
do they only sleep
in cold arms of earth
deaf to morning bells
or do they hear a voice
calling each by name?

One Incarnation

Marilyn Gear Pilling

Like a church spire you are all
Verticals today, your
Body a charged wire
On the rack that runs
Between heaven and hell.
No horizontal planes to your
Psyche or soma, you seem
A figure from El Greco
All anguished angularity.
When you rise to read, the
Wide, deep collar of your shirt is
Turned up; even it stands tall
Chafes your earlobes into starch.
God cranks.
The Devil cranks.
Before my eyes you grow
Thinner and thinner, headed for
Allegory.

Some Mystery Must Remain

Marilyn Gear Pilling

Beside me, a strawberry blonde and her licorice brunet
    lover, his hand on her thigh, his arm closely coated
with hairs of shiny black. Her arm beside his, soft fuzzy
    peach in the sacred light that streams from the notes of
Lamentations and Praises, Learned of Angel, Sanctus.

She shifts position, her culotte slides up, reveals a leg
   so hirsute, black hairs so thick and so coarse
I seem to be viewing an animal's pelt. Though the foot
   at the end of the limb is shod in a white, flowered
shoe, I follow the line of the leg to see if somehow

it belongs to the boyfriend brunet—it doesn't, of
course—
   then crane to check the roots of her hair, her brows
her lashes behind glasses—all true strawberry blonde.
   Dona Nobis Pacem, Agnus Dei, The Awakening -
in the midst of Spirit, this irruption of feral leg.

Every Station of the Cross

Marilyn Gear Pilling

You have made a cross from a tree
and it hangs behind you
as you read your poem in fourteen parts.
Above you hangs the concrete cross
that is always in this church.
You noticed your cross
in the shape of a tree
that was part of an orchard destroyed
for a mall, and is now the subject
of your poem for every station of the cross.

Her torso curves like a crescent moon
this cross you found in a tree
who hangs behind you as you read.
You have stripped her of her bark
rubbed her body until it shines oak gold.

Where her arms join her torso,
a knothole. Below,
a schism runs to her feet;
her arms point east and west.
Near the wrist, her left arm becomes two
diverges like the path in the yellow wood.

As you read she begins to move
this being you found in a felled
tree, moves her body
to your cadence. Her arms beckon
the east, beckon the west.
The split that runs from knothole down
becomes a stream, vineyards appear
along its banks *and the vines*
with the tender grape give a good smell.
All eyes are on her. Behind you
she is leafing green and gold.

Flora's Bread

Marilyn Gear Pilling

In December, my mother's sister baked her last
loaves, lay down and died in her sleep.

The crust of the bread was burnt
its form was fallen, misshapen.

That Christmas, my mother asked me—
Would you take some of Flora's bread?

I have her last batch in my freezer;

would you take two loaves of her bread?

No thanks, I told her
I have my own.

Would you like just one loaf?
It's Flora's bread.

No thanks. I have my own bread.
I don't eat other kinds.

The next year, like her sister
my mother died in December.

Oh loaf of bread, if ever
you come again in my lifetime,

I will take you, will bow my head,
kiss your burnt crust

I will break you, taste you, savour
your whole center, your scarred breadth.

Oh loaf of bread,
forgive me.

Dear God

Marilyn Gear Pilling

Let it be twilight, for only then do you paint like Matisse.

Let the sky's daring be a chromatic red, daubs of orange
and gold.
           Let Kiri be singing O mio babbino caro.
                Let the speed of my car be 180 k.
                  Let it leave the earth.

Give me a second or two to understand the levitation
      as inevitable
           so I may add to it my power
             my submission.

And in the years before this event
      roll me, oh God
           roll me in the glorious mess of life
               the guts the mud the smite the
               blood the song the sob
                  of life.

Roll me as I roll the dough of the leavened bread.
      Kneed me, God.
           Pummel me.
              Press me thin.

Set me to rise in warm places.
      Use me up

so that when the flying is over, when the crash comes,
      your fire has only my crumbs
           to burn

for the rest of me has sown itself into your world
into every little crevice and rockface
into each particular heartscape
of this fallen world.

Attentive Waiting—A Conversation Concerning Conversion

John B. Lee

"I used to think I was put on this earth for one purpose alone. I was placed here to grow corn. And I was more than content with my lot. I thought I loved my life. I enjoyed and was satisfied and took my meaning and the sole meaning of my existence from the nurturing of this weak, hybrid, cultivated, pampered, green little plant."

These were the words of my cousin, that day, in the gentle picnic rain on a summer Sunday, sitting outside the shadow of the shelter in lawn chairs in a small consanguinary circle of maternal family. They certainly weren't common to our talk. Although rooted in farming, as most conversations were with us, these words were throwing their seed over the wall and falling on fallow, in the metaphysical rural, rain-rich earth of land beyond our lives.

"I was so obsessed with my crop, I used to time myself between farms. I'd seek and find short cuts, quick roads, paths to shave a few seconds off arrival so that I could be there in the field. I'd go walking the rows. I'd know each plant among thousands as a prosperous man might know his many children. I'd instruct my young workers. Give them heart to tassel. Hope to harvest. Don't stand at the start of your row and despair for the multitudes before you, but rather, stay where you are—then, when you're there, stand at each stalk and be present in the silk of your doing the work at hand. Then your day will be done, your labour complete, the hours full. And they listened."

"Each year came. Each season required. In the winter, I thought of the spring. In the spring, I outwaited the frost and the wet. I was patient with land. I worked it like weather. I watched while my neighbours broke ground too soon. They just couldn't learn."

"And then, one day, five years ago, my daughter gave birth to a son who no one thought would survive. I'd be there in London, simply waiting and waiting. I'd be thinking of home and the work of the world. I'd leave the hospital and speed to the field where I mounted the tractor and worked. But at each round of the headland, at each culvert and turn of the ditch, at each force of the fence, I'd feel the wheel turning toward London taking me back to that bedside, back to that vigil."

"You have to know—I could do nothing but be there. But I was compelled by the feeling that I had never done anything more important in my life than that. I was simply waiting. There was nothing I could say. Nothing I could actually do to make any real difference. I was never more helpless. Nor have I ever done a better thing."

"I had thought my purpose in life was to grow corn. It took me over fifty years to learn that the most important thing I had ever done was to simply be there. To be present. To engage in that attentive waiting."

"I suppose I had been compelled by a fruitless obsession all my life. Now I know, the true heroes are those who are willing to give up everything for what really matters. To be there for others. To simply wait and do nothing was the greatest and most heroic and best thing I have ever done."

"And the learning of that lesson is the greatest gift I have ever received," he said.

Tomorrow he waits again.

The Conspiracy

Robert Hill

It seemed a final contradiction—
   his watch, still running,
   the memory of the years
   frozen by the moving hands.
He had been assured by regulations:
household routine, the morning news, his dinner hour
   predictable from day to day.
He could not understand the logic of time
   as human invention.
"The minutes drive the hours," he would say
    "the hours drive the days.
   We live by regulation."
The summation of his final years was simple:
"We come into the world on time. We leave on time."
Minutes, hours, days—he never got beyond it.
   So. I was asked:
   "Would you like his watch?"
The second hand ticked away its rhythm
moving through the measureless infinity.
   I envisioned eternity
regulated by the cadence of my father's watch.
   All things ordered—
the cycle of seasons, the movement of tides,
precise dates for births, deaths, all natural events.
   I considered the implications.
   "No. Leave it with him. Leave it."
   It's a comfort to know
   there's something there in charge.

Marquis Book Printing Inc.

Québec, Canada
2008